USAIN BOLT

Roy Apps

Illustrated by Chris King

LONDON · SYDNEY

Franklin Watts
First published in Great Britain in 2016
by The Watts Publishing Group

Text © Roy Apps 2016
Illustrations © Chris King 2016
Cover design by Peter Scoulding

PB ISBN 978 1 4451 4142 8
ebook ISBN 978 1 4451 4143 5
Library ebook ISBN 978 1 4451 4144 2

3 5 7 9 10 8 6 4

Printed in Great Britain

MIX
Paper from
responsible sources
FSC® C104740
FSC
www.fsc.org

Franklin Watts
An imprint of
Hachette Children's Group
Part of The Watts Publishing Group
Carmelite House
50 Victoria Embankment
London EC4Y 0DZ

An Hachette UK Company
www.hachette.co.uk

www.franklinwatts.co.uk

Chapter One:

Let's Go, Go, Go!

Usain was out in the Jamaican bush with only his dog Brownie for company. The bush was a huge area of tall trees and thick scrub: just right for imagining yourself as a superhero, tracking down a gang of criminals. It was also a dangerous kind of place. It was so vast you could get lost and no one would know where you were. Usain knew that he would be in really big trouble if his dad ever found out that he'd been playing there. Which meant that he needed to be home before his dad got back from work.

Suddenly, Brownie's ears pricked up. He'd heard something. Usain tensed and watched as the dog listened some more. Brownie barked, then raced off through the bushes. For Usain, that bark was

like the bang of a starting gun: he knew
he'd got to run. What Brownie had
heard was the sound of Usain's dad's
motorbike on its way home.

"Yo, boy!" yelled Usain to Brownie.
"Let's go, go, go!"

Usain and Brownie crashed through
the undergrowth until they reached
the dirt road, then they sprinted home.
Outside the front door, Usain quickly
grabbed a cricket ball. He pretended
to be practising his fast bowling, just
as his dad's ancient motorbike skidded
round the corner. His dad switched off
the engine and waved to Usain.

"Still at the cricket practice, Bolt?"
Usain's dad always called him Bolt.

"Oh, hi, Pops!" Usain pretended to look
surprised to see him.

Usain's dad went into the house. "Good boy," Usain whispered to Brownie, patting him on the head. "Looks like you and I made it back home just in time. Thanks to you having the best hearing of any dog in the village." He paused, then grinned. "Mind you, me being the fastest kid in the village helped, too!"

Chapter Two:

Mesmerised

Usain was the fastest kid in the village. And he had a dream: to use his speed to become a fast bowler for the West Indies, like his hero and fellow Jamaican, the West Indies cricket captain, Courtney Walsh.

Usain was looking forward to starting high school. He'd enjoyed primary school, but he knew that at high school he would have the chance to play proper cricket with proper cricket coaches. But he was in for a big shock.

A few weeks into his first term at high school, he strolled out onto the cricket pitch at the start of that day's PE lesson. He practised a few run-ups and then the PE teacher came over to him.

"Sorry, Bolt," he said, "no more cricket for you. Get yourself over to the running track."

"Why, sir?" protested Usain.

"Because running is what you're best at," the teacher replied.

So Usain switched to running. He did well, winning the school championship and getting a trophy to prove it. But

because he was so tall and naturally talented, he didn't really have to try. He never really worked at training and often he'd skip it altogether.

One evening, after Usain had missed training again, his coach decided that enough was enough. He stormed off into town, looking for Usain. He found him in a café, chatting up some girls. He took him outside.

"I am so seriously fed up with you, Bolt!" he thundered.

Usain shrugged. "Hey, man, I won the school championship, didn't I? I don't need all this training hassle."

"School championship?" replied the coach angrily. "Bolt, have you no idea just how good you could be if you really put your heart into it? Forget the school champs. With your natural

11

talent you could be looking at medals at international level."

Next week, Usain turned up for training.

"We're going to do things differently today, Bolt," his coach said.

"Yeah?"

"Yeah. Instead of racing round the track, you and I are gonna watch some TV. Sit down and put your feet up."

Usain and his coach watched a video of the 1996 Olympic Games. Usain saw the crowds shouting and cheering as US sprinter Michael Johnson powered home to win first the 200 metres and then the 400 metres gold.

He was mesmerised. "Man, that's what I want to do!" he declared. "Win a gold medal at the Olympic Games!"

Chapter Three:

Bolt! Bolt! Lightning Bolt!

The next Olympic Games were in 2000 in Sydney, Australia. But while the world's athletes got ready for this global event, Usain was busy training hard for the 2001 Regional Schools'

200 metres at the National Stadium in Kingston.

The training paid off. Although Usain's long legs meant he was slow out of the starting blocks, he managed to catch the leader on the bend and power home in first place. As he stepped up onto the podium to cheers from the crowd, he discovered he rather liked winning.

Still only 15, Usain was picked for the 2001 Caribbean Junior Competition in Barbados and then chosen to represent Jamaica at the World Youth Championships in Hungary, where he reached the semi-finals.

He should have been full of confidence, but he wasn't. His next event was going to be a really big one: the World Juniors.

"I don't think I'm ready for this," he told his coach.

"Why not?" asked his coach.

"There are going to be guys running who are 18 and 19 — way older than me. I don't need this hassle. I'm not going."

"You'll do just great," his coach assured him.

"And another thing," Usain added.
"It's taking place down the road —
in Kingston!"

"So you won't have far to travel," his
coach reasoned.

"Yeah, but it'll be a home crowd!"

"You have a problem with that?" asked his coach.

"Sure, man! They'll all be expecting me to win! I'm likely to be the only Jamaican in the final. Suppose I mess it up?"

It was Usain's mum who persuaded him to change his mind.

"Just go, son. Do your best. Whatever the result we'll be proud of you. And another thing, your family will be there to cheer you on!"

Usain worked hard with his coach, going to the gym, running, exercising, anything to take his mind off the fast-approaching World Juniors.

It was only when he walked into the Kingston stadium on the day of the World Junior 200 metres, that Usain

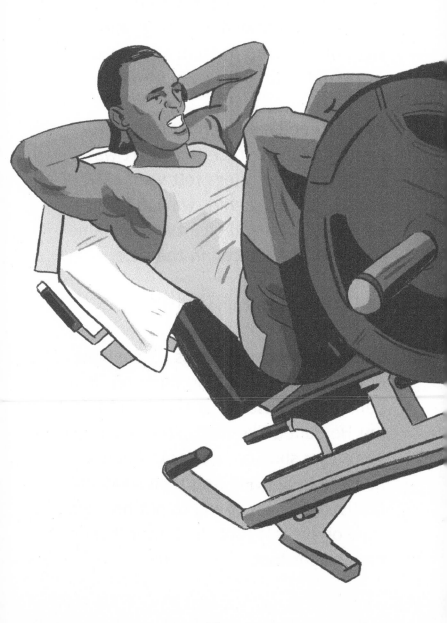

realised just how big the event was. It was an international meeting, and the sight of TV cameras from all over the world did nothing to calm his nerves.

By the time Usain went trackside to warm up for the race, his heart was pounding and his legs felt weak. The crowd was going wild, waving flags, banging drums and chanting the name of the only Jamaican in the race:

"Bolt! Bolt! Lightning Bolt!"

Shaking with nervousness, Usain bent down to put his running shoes on. In a panic, he realised that they wouldn't go on! He pulled like mad. Still he couldn't get either shoe on. He looked down at them in despair. And then suddenly realised...he was trying to put his right shoe on his left foot, and his left shoe on his right foot.

Only when he got to the starting blocks, did he start to calm down.

Bang! went the starter's gun.

As ever, Usain was slow out of the blocks, but then he powered forward, his long strides taking him past the rest of the field.

As he neared the finishing line, he glanced back. There were no other runners in sight. He crossed the line first: the World Junior 200 metres champion.

"Bolt! Bolt! Lightning Bolt!" roared the crowd.

A Jamaican flag was thrown onto the track. Usain draped it round his shoulders, then ran towards the crowd and saluted them, military style.

There was no doubt about it: Usain Bolt was a star. Not only was he the World Junior 200 metres champion, he was also the youngest-ever World Junior gold medallist.

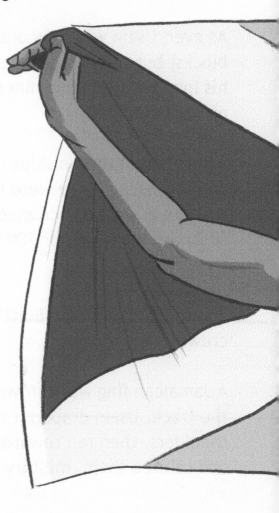

Chapter Four:

Pain

"You know what I think, Bolt?" Usain's coach said. "I think you can go to the 2004 Olympics in Athens and bag a medal."

"Yeah?" grinned Usain. He thought back to the day when he had first seen the video of Michael Johnson winning gold at the Atlanta Games. Ever since then he had dreamt of winning an Olympic medal.

"What are we waiting for then, coach?" said Usain. "Let's get down to business!"

It wasn't easy. Following his triumph at the World Juniors, Usain had moved to Kingston, the capital and largest city in Jamaica, so that he could train at the IAAF High Performance Centre there. Life in the city was very different to the life he had known growing up in a small village out in the bush. He began to go partying big-time. And when he wasn't partying there were the cafés, dance halls and carnival nights. There were always plenty of girls who wanted a date with a World Junior champion and national hero.

Eventually, Usain's coach put his foot

down. "Bolt, you're meant to be a pro athlete! Just get your act together and stop fooling around! Otherwise you'll have no chance in Athens."

There was no way Usain wanted to miss out on a chance of a medal in Athens. He knuckled down to some serious training and, with a heavy heart, quit the Kingston party scene.

The months of gruelling hard work seemed to pay off when, in the junior CARIFTA Games in 2004, he broke the 200 metres World Junior Record with a time of 19.93 seconds. Athens was only a few months away, and Usain was at the top of his game.

A couple of weeks later he was on the track doing a few practice laps when suddenly he was gripped by stabbing pain in the back of his leg. He crashed to the ground in agony.

Usain travelled to Germany to see a doctor who specialised in leg and back injuries. After the examination, Usain could tell by the expression on the doctor's face that it was bad news. "Mr Bolt," he said, "I'm afraid your spine is the wrong shape. It's like an S. That is why you have suffered this injury."

In the few weeks left leading up to the Athens Olympic Games, Usain took a special fitness programme to try and deal with the problem in his back and to ease the pain.

Although he managed to get fit enough to take part in the Olympics, he was nowhere near fit enough to run a good race. He was eliminated in the heats.

Things looked bleak. Could it be that his professional career as an athlete was over?

Chapter Five:

Champion's Run?

When Usain got back home to Jamaica there were no flags, no drums, no cheering crowds. Instead, people were muttering to each other:

"Bolt's lost it..."

"Can't take the pressure of a big event..."

"He's just a lazy kid..."

In a way, they were right. Usain was just a kid: he'd had his eighteenth birthday during the Olympics. He felt worn out by training and deep down, he was worried about his injuries. If he was going to make it as a runner, he decided, he needed a new start: and a new start meant a new coach.

Usain's new coach was Glen Mills.

"Bolt," he said, "you have talent, but we need to take things slowly so that you can be ready for the 2008 Beijing Olympics."

"Beijing! That's four years away!" protested Usain. "I'll be twenty-two by then!"

"So?" Coach Mills replied, with a shrug. "That hardly makes you an old person, does it?"

Coach Mills's new training regime suited Usain well. He did gym work to strengthen the muscles in his legs and a masseur was brought in to help with his back problem. By the time the 2005

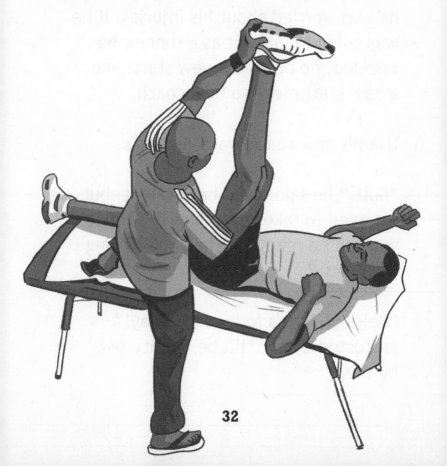

World Championships came round he felt ready for the challenge. He came first in the heats. When it came to the final, he was off like a shot with the crack of the starter's gun and ahead of the pack at the turn.

"Yo!" Usain thought to himself, excitedly. "The power of the Lightning Bolt is back! You could be on for a championship medal here, man!"

He pushed hard to put more distance between himself and the pack. But, in his excitement, he pushed too hard. Suddenly, he felt the familiar pain grip the back of his leg. His hamstring had torn. "I'm not pulling out," he muttered to himself. "I'll finish this race, whatever."

Usain managed to jog the rest of the way painfully to the line. He finished last.

As he came off the track, he looked up and saw Coach Mills smiling at him.

"Coach, what are you grinning at?" Usain asked, despondently.

Coach Mills shrugged. "Bolt, you showed what you are made of out there! Despite your hamstring going, you didn't quit! Bolt, I saw you running your heart out today. That was a true champion's run."

Usain studied Coach Mills hard. "I come last and you're happy? What are you? A crazy man?"

"No," replied Coach Mills. "I'm a man who believes you have the makings of a true champion!"

Chapter Six:

The Fastest Man on Earth

Once again, Usain set off on the long road of recovery from injury. After rest and recuperation he started his training schedule again. Within a year he had climbed back into the world top five rankings.

The following year, 2007, he won the 200 metres silver medal at the World Championships in Osaka, Japan. Seven months later, in May 2008, he broke the 100 metres world record in a time of 9.72 seconds. He was now officially "The Fastest Man On Earth". He was ready for the Olympic Games.

The first few days of the Olympics were quiet ones for Usain. He was just another one of the hundreds of athletes who had gathered in Beijing for the biggest sporting event in the world.

He got through the heats and semi-finals comfortably. The 100 metres final was to take place just a couple of hours after the end of the semis.

Usain warmed down to keep his muscles working, then his masseur set to work on his back, hips and ankles. He felt relaxed. So relaxed, that he decided to play a joke on his coach.

As Coach Mills gave him a reassuring squeeze of the shoulder, Usain crumpled to the ground with a terrifying scream. He pretended to writhe in agony. The cameras zoomed in. "Breaking news! Usain Bolt's been injured by his coach!"

Usain got up, laughing. Everyone cheered; everyone that is, except Coach Mills.

The runners got to the starting blocks and the crowd fell silent.

Bang! went the starter's gun.

Usain was off, but it wasn't a good start. In no time at all though, his

strong legs powered him forward
and soon he was leading the pack.
At 80 metres, he looked back over his
shoulder and saw that he was way, way
out in front. At 90 metres, he slowed
down. He was celebrating before he'd
even crossed the line.

It was mayhem. As the photographers crowded round him he pulled back his arm and aimed it upwards towards the sky: a lightning bolt.

Not only had Usain won the 100 metres gold, he had broken his own world

record. But he didn't stop there. He went on to win the 200 metres and then, with his Jamaican team-mates, the 4 x 100 metres relay. All in record time.

The first thing Usain did once all the fuss was over was to sit down and watch a video of himself winning Olympic gold. Just as, all those years ago, he'd sat and watched Michael Johnson winning gold at the 1996 Olympic Games.

When they got back to Jamaica, Coach Mills asked Usain, "How's it feel to be The Fastest Man on Earth and a triple Olympic champion then, Bolt?"

"Yeah, kinda cool," replied Usain with a grin. "But I reckon I could go a stage further. I reckon I could become a legend."

Four years later at the next Olympic Games, in London, Usain Bolt became the first man in history to defend both the 100 metres and 200 metres titles. At the end of the 200 metres final, he did five press-ups — one for each of his Olympic Gold medals, so far.

Usain Bolt had indeed become a legend.

Fact file
Usain Bolt

Full name: Usain St Leo Bolt

Born: 21 August 1986, Sherwood Content, Trelawny, Jamaica

Height: 1.96 metres

Medals

— 2002 World Junior Championships
200m Gold

— 2003 World Youth Championships
200m Gold

— 2006 World Athletic Final
200m Bronze

— IAAF World Cup
200m Silver

— 2007 World Championships
200m Silver
4 x 100m Relay Silver

— 2008 Olympic Games
100m Gold
200m Gold
4 x 100m Relay Gold

— 2009 World Championships
200m Gold
4 x 100m Relay

— 2011 World Championships
200m Gold
4 x 100m Relay Gold

— 2012 Olympic Games
100m Gold
200m Gold
4 x 100m Relay Gold

— 2013 World Championships
100m Gold
200m Gold
4 x 100m Relay Gold

— 2014 Commonwealth Games
4 x 100m Relay Gold

— 2015 World Championships
100m Gold
200m Gold
4 x 100m Relay Gold

Nicola Adams

At the Sports Centre, Nicola's mum went off to her aerobics class while her brother Kurtis quickly found his way to football training. A sports coach came over to Nicola.

"What about you, young lady?" he asked. "What would you like to have a go at? Dance, perhaps?"

Nicola frowned and shook her head. "I want to do boxing," she said.

"Boxing?" the coach repeated with a snort. "You're a girl! Girls don't box..." Then he saw the determined look on Nicola's face. He knew straight away it would be no good arguing with her.

Continue reading this story in:
DREAM TO WIN:
Nicola Adams